Soaring

Jack Oats

Soaring

Soaring
ISBN 978 1 76041 411 5
Copyright © text Jack Oats 2017
Cover photo: white-bellied sea eagle, Ford Kristo

First published 2017 by
GINNINDERRA PRESS
PO Box 3461 Port Adelaide 5015 Australia
www.ginninderrapress.com.au

Contents

Introductions	9
A day in the life of an atheist	12
Jack Oats	14
Resolve	15
Being, Birding, Birds	17
Dearest MakMak people	19
Welcome to Country	20
Green catbird	22
The English blackbird	23
Dawn chorus	25
Another dawn chorus	26
Pipers at dusk	27
Desert totem	28
Wedding photos in the park	32
Bliss on a houseboat	33
Cicadabird	34
Painted snipe	35
Secrets	36
Dreams	39
Dream waves	41
A proper goodbye	42
Still life	43
Reconciliation Day	44
Fogged in on the Bridge	45
Kosciuszko	46
In search of the dreaming colour	47
Edge trilogy	48
Scarlet's waltz	50
Epyllion for Sydney	53
Tripping with an angel	56
From the watchtower	59

On lost children — 61
- Daughter — 63
- Missing boy — 64
- Helicopter — 65
- Gaunt epigones — 66
- Giving up light — 67
- Song from Keleni — 68
- On the bright side — 70

On trains and the occasional bus and ferry — 71
- The Ghan — 73
- Tourist haikus en route to Yellow Water river cruise — 74
- Watching him, watching them — 75
- Whazisname from the commuters' club — 76
- Orienteering in the suburbs — 77
- The train home — 78
- The bloke at the station — 80
- White Christmas on Route 184 — 82
- Ballad of solicitation — 83

On love — 85
- Natural selection — 87
- Oyster Bay — 88
- Moonlight and adults tarry — 90
- The kiss — 91
- Fantasia — 92
- The fifteen-year rule — 93
- A rose — 94
- With what's left — 95
- Love again — 96
- Moondancer — 97
- To be left on the shelf — 98

Random stuff — 99
- A short history of animals — 101
- Air — 102

In the Simpson Desert	103
Blocked images from 1588	104
Cynical exercise	105
Frescos revealed	106
Huntsman's sea change	107
In three steps	108
Petrified wood	109
Janet	110
Jhomolhari spirit	112
Pop's fob watch	114
Silence	115
Shadow racer	116
Saturday morning is all right	118
The quoll song	120
The girters' anthem	122

For seniors — 125

A (little) bloke's look	127
It's not cricket	128
Pre-op	129
Mettle detector	130
On coiling	132
On composting	133
Requited love atop Lady Barrington	134
Pre-breakfast snack	135
To remember two	136
Tenet of place	138
A farewell hug	139
Widow at evensong	140
Winter surfer	141
Sunset clause	142

Acknowledgements	143
Sea eagle	145

For my grandchildren

I am the words you take from me

Introductions

Each time, a single spider reconfobulates in the centre of my vision. Eyes tightly closed, I imperceptibly adjust direction and distance then snap my eyes open but there's no tricking them; one is central to my vision as it slowly hoists up on an invisible thread and melts into the ceiling. Mostly they're huge hairy-legged huntsman, although the paler ones are cloaked in dozens of feathery-down appendages that help them float upwards; perhaps they're birds not spiders. My right thumb finds the small button with the green backlighting and another drop of morphine is delivered intravenously. The next time I snap open my eyes, no spider. Instead, tiny black ant-dots slide across a ceiling panel, congregate as if funnelled into a corner, then disappear. Green light, thumb action and now multiple spiders and ant-dots.

Briefly, fully conscious, I can discern between the hallucinations and the routine activities in the cardiac intensive care unit, although everything is surreal. In a moment of lucidity, I vow that if I survive, I will compile my first collection of poems into a book. And I think a little prayer.

A day in the life of an atheist

early Matins
acknowledge rising Sun
asking only for peace
goodwill among people
and they with holy Earth

> no outward sign
> no star to wear
> no sacred wine
> no cross to bear

thanksgiving at Vespers
knowing always the Earth
held close as answered prayer
and sometimes asking for
another day

Laughter, mates, family, creativity and the privilege of having lived in Australia in peace and affluence, these are serious matters. Most important for me, having survived to be sixty-seven, including the recent heart attack and heart surgery, is not to take myself too seriously. So, by way of introduction:

Jack Oats

'Bake!' exclaims his old history teacher, 'I remember you on the wing
in Smithy's team.' After fifty years the name still fixed in his mind.

But not with Jack. It had only stuck those last two years of school.
Those were the days before nicknames went out of vogue,

while he was becoming titled 'Sir' and 'Daddy' then 'Dad'
and later, 'JB', 'Granjack', 'Doctor' and 'Boss'.

In between, he dabbled with a home-handyman business and
as a joke he was Jack Oats (Of All TradeS).

So the CV mentions teacher, tradie, ornithologist, consultant,
biologist, bureaucrat and all-round bull-shitter
but never once 'baker'.

In the family tree there's a carpenter, wheelwright, horse-trader,
boilermakers and an ironmonger's assistant,
Ebenezer Samuel Baker, b. c. 1870, Launceston, England.

And all along, John Baker after his father and his father
to satisfy convention and the Electoral Office;

Richard (middle name) because his mother liked it. He never did
(dreading the standard nickname) but he loved her.

Now, on the wings of a sea eagle and with a prayer of resurrection
for the semicolon, soars Jack Oats the poet.

Resolve

with each new year comes
resolve to sculpture anew
the block we call life

Being, Birding, Birds

Dearest MakMak people

Like you, I am of the sea eagle.
That bird is my totem.
When my gubba-heart is heavy,
a polished stone in the river
or beach-cast,
my eyes search the sky
and hope is there.
The MakMak is my solace.

There: I have stolen your word.

Like you, I'm bereft.
My children were taken too
and when my anger rages
against the cruelty of fate, the cruelty
of people there is no kind way to accept,
my mind aches for reasons
and drifts away over the ocean.
The MakMak is my strength.

There: a word to use for my feelings.

Like you, I yearn for place.
You struggled and kept your place
but I've always been lost: no fragment
of history, of clan; stories, myths abandoned.
My connection with dragon slayers,
lions and the rose is frayed
so please, don't you exclude me.
The MakMak can be a beginning.

Your word is here, a song for me.

Welcome to Country

Sunrise
winter solstice
after weeks immersed in
        alone
the calm and calming
my dreams within dreaming
              your place

Then a brush of riffled air
the hum of a shadow over my hat
your wings outstretched
gaze friendly
        Bunjil

A subordinate male
sent by your people
you stand and face me
solemn, I bow;
your nod is formal
I walk on
you circle just above the ground
wings tipping ahead of me
see emu rushing back and forth
indecision or auspicion
again you circle ahead
wing tips pointing
see plenty kangaroo
none of them hurry

'And then he floats low over his land
vanishing back into the desert!'
(husky whisper, Cambridge accent)

An Attenborough moment
and I don't mind dignifying him
by including him in it

You know?
         we'll never belong here
in the Country of the Eagle
but this morning I understood
                acceptance

Green catbird

for novice birdwatchers
rainforest is tricky
with neck bending up and
binoculars ready
you strain for a glimpse through
the shadows and speckles
birds feeding, catcalling
miaowing their heckles

The English blackbird

11 November 2011

There's a new irritation:
not another Royals media hype
not the lost spectacles again
not the slow greying of hair
or wrinkling of skin
not the same old weeds
we've battled for years
nor the house sparrow.
We grew up with sparrows.

It's a sudden shock
striking like toothache, earache,
rheumatism or gout;
like the McMansions
springing up in our street
an invasion of our neighbourhood
a taunting threat to peace and sanity
the British effrontery of it.

This is worse than:
spelling eczema haemorrhoids tinnitus
being put *on hold* by Telstra again
intrusive mobile phone users
our scandalous local councillors.
By comparison, the Indian mynah
seems like an old friend.
We'll remove the No Junk sign
from our letter box and
be polite to Jehovah's Witnesses.

The blackbird is a bully and a Kerr.
Wrens and honeyeaters have been expelled
while it skulks in the vegie patch
destroying lettuce seedlings, murdering worms
and worst insult to our decades of bush-care
its nest despoiling our native garden.

With defiant hubris it calls
from our prized Illawarra flame tree.
Nemesis! Oh just goddess.
No armistice:
rid our paradise of this new enemy.

Dawn chorus

Dawn creeps
fingers extending to tickle kookaburras
and, as Sydney wakes, the full moon concedes
sinking low beneath cloud covers.

Bamboo wind chimes chortle
at wakeful bladders
and in the mountains, Kendall's birds
ring alarm bells.

Suburban trains rattle commuters' sleep.
From TV antennas, magpies wardle-doodle early news and warnings.
High above, crammed with suit-wearers,
the grumble of sky-pencils scraping lines that join cities.

Black cockatoos whinge about the weather.
The rain falls softly.
Sally barks once without commitment
and returns to kennel.

Silver gulls squark objections to the cold southerly.
A listless tide tucks over the shore,
Pelicans drift overhead,
Sandman, subliminal says, 'Stay in bed.'

Another dawn chorus

A winter-crisp silence
expands to the horizon.
Red kangaroos silhouetted
still and tall, ears twitching.
Hovering kestrels listen in a void
for the movement of shadows.
A wagtail waits low on a mulga bush.
Woodswallows huddle breathless on a baton

anticipating the first glimmer
of a piano concerto;
Brahms's second comes to mind.
In one frozen moment
the desert greets the sun
the silence is done.

Pipers at dusk

Straining to hear them against
the grumble of ocean
breeze ruffling heath
my chattering teeth
rain on hat
the noisy raincoat
swishing away insects
buzzing around my ears
an early owl and
the call of a warm dry tent.

The survey sheet shows nothing
of the noisy wilderness static
crowding in with the dark
nor the ecstasy of those first ascending notes
rippling over Nadgee Moor.

Then the pencil pandemonium
beginning at 1842 hrs
32 minutes after sunset
7 minutes of mapping 200 calls
counting 13 birds
two seen flying as they call.

The survey sheets are filed and there's a publication
'*Managing the ground parrot*
in its fiery habitat in south-eastern Australia'
with barely a hint of their allure.

Desert totem

for Norma

1 *the birder*

The tapestry of tapestries
of time of place of being
of soaring over it all after rain
looking down and sensing
desert form, desert life.

It's meant to be dry and harsh
now bizarrely green and lush.
Red threads of sand dunes
parallel then meeting
singular then unravelling
spreading then merging with the swales
that reduce them to pinstripes
threatening to clothe them
with greens imagined
by a weaver obsessed with
the variety of water colours.
A myriad of braided streams
crimped and fraying string-lines
their ornate waltzes etched into
ancient rock-solid dirt
by decadal desert water flows
converging on, spilling from salt pans.
Dry white lakes become a palette
mirror wet reflecting brown mauve silver
silken crescents of iridescent yellow
fringed with red and greens.

On a low ridge a rock wallaby stands defiant
among the angles made by
dark creases on the earth's crust
and splodges of freshly washed colour
on time-worn escarpments
glinting with metallic oxides grey orange blue.

Green on green collage
as far as the eye can see
until we glide over the horizon
to the parched place of a rain shadow
or the threadbare summer after next
with no rain in between
or a fire-ravaged land
where lightning strikes put paid to
the extravagant build up of life.

2 *the bird*

Together on this flight but not entwined
over the centre of a desert continent
your shadow speeds across the ground below me
you are the silver bird highest in the sky
you are passing over but you don't belong
with the desert.
You see delicate vignettes
softly filigreed edges
gently textured sculptures.
You don't sight perentie waiting to kill wallaby
you're not overpowered
by the boiling perfume of so many flowers
the icy silence of desert nights
the merciless rent of rock tooth talon.

We understand so little of each other
but you call me black-breasted.
What can you see of me from on high?
Do you see my rich rufous neck
the intricate lacework of my feather tips
do you appreciate my discerning eye
and what do you know of my heart
is your heart black on the inside?

Hearts are as they must be
strong reliable efficient machines.
Yours are enormous silver beads
strung along your wings as you roar overhead.
My heart soars in silence
an enduring warm pink-gold
quilted with black embroidery.
Life. It's not about the good times
lush deserts, satiated senses.
The harshest times are meant for survivors.

Think of me as
dreamy in the hardest of places
fore-thoughtful hunter of beauty
the meta-tapestry of seasons
reject that buzzard name you copy from the books.
If you must know me
call me Heart of the Desert.

Wedding photos in the park

for Thyra

Sheets of rain flap wildly
white on back-lit clouds
reflecting grey in ephemeral lakes.

At the breakfast feast, drunken ravens strut:
the groom and men in their dark suits
bloat on worms in watery soup.

In stilettos, the fastidious bride and maids:
the egret and herons twist their long necks
gawk and pick at delicacies.

Animated specks join the wedding party:
silver gulls, not confetti.

Bliss on a houseboat

Late afternoon moored
in Little Shark Rock Bay.
Twin angophoras float by,
their orange pink-grey trunks
smudged across the deep green,
then swing back,
their dense broccoli heads
of bright lime foliage
harbouring the brassy *krish rish*
of an overdosed cicada; the greengrocer.
Through bloodshot eyes
he watches our slow eddying
and krishes undeterred by the drizzle.
Now, glossy black-cockatoos mooch by
fanning red tails
and bemoaning last year's poor seed-set.
With their grating *skeeet keeet*
they flop among the tops
of casuarinas drifting
upturned in the mirror of our bay.

Cicadabird

All that time spent
chasing you
your call teasing.
Years of hoping
just to glimpse the
krish-rish-rish bird.
The books call you
'common migrant'.
Why so shy?

Now, two-thousand
miles from home
and
without a word,
you perch in clear view;
I am alone.
You are sleek
perfect.
My life (list) is changed.

Painted snipe

Rain on fogged binoculars,
boots bogged in the marshland,
and still, we attack the place.
We're loud, belligerent,
possessed. A disgrace
until finally

the snipe, glimpsed briefly,
its face pouting, eyebrow raised,
beak long, upturned, sharp
with rapid-fire call;
the snipe, on skittish wings,
departs the cluttered canvas.

Too slow, birdie! There's now a red dot
on the picture of you in our books.

Secrets

for Les, the bloke who knows forest secrets

    Above the roar of your silence
leaves whisper, unseen in the canopy
    In vale below, the quiet tinkle of birds
and deeper in the silence, a river
    Seek the smallest micro-bats in the hollows of the greatest of trees
kept awake by incessant cicadas
    Behind the moon, owls emerge from forest giants
to scream warnings, then hunt noiselessly
    In swamps multilingual refrains of froggies go a-courting
ah-hum, ah-hum, ah-humah-humah-hum
their nuptial pads a-ready for gripping
slippery strangers in the night
the mottling is python intent on amphibian
    A vine stretches translucent tendrils, flesh-pale support for
glossy leaves reflecting black on a steamy precipice
    Do lyrebirds imitate cuckoos, those mistresses of deceit
the raucous screams of stormbirds
or the granny-sweet whistle of its tiny shining cousin
    Better perhaps to count funereal cockatoos and hope for rainy days
these blackened stumps and trunks tell of fire and destruction
    Butterflies chase shameless butterflies
sumptuous white petals of bridal orchids coy in the ferny undergrowth
and more shy, the tree orchid trailing faint-green fronds
and delicate sprays of gold down the trunk of an old river sheoak
    Precious life, sweetest water from an icy mountain stream
(and you've remembered the chocolate!)

    Smell Gondwana on the damp floor of an ancient beech forest
the spore-laden breath of fungi seeps from
inverted caps full of lacy-white frills
a bunch have threads for stems and red button tops with white dots
    Tall tall gums
bark shedding and smooth trunks that glow crimson at sunrise
deep shade and deep peace at midday
a patch of filtered light for a basking velvet lizard
and wattle seedling stretching up
    The rolling summits retiring in the clouds
vine-tangled treetops shrouded in fine mist that evaporates to show
in startling clarity: the forest is every green

    A robin pipes sweet and soft
what other secrets have you, forest?

Dreams

Dream waves

    the thing
with dreams is the
discontinuities.
From normal to mayhem like 'that'.
Instant

the thing
with dreams is the
reality. Pleasures
but more often pain and there's no
escape

    the thing
with dreams is the
edits. You can rewind
manipulate rerun and yet
chaos

the thing
with dreams is the
fear that poisons your mind.
By the time you're awake it is
too late

    and yet
with our babies
we hug them every night
and croon in prayer for them and us
'sweet dreams'

A proper goodbye

For how many years must I dream
the sight of your wrinkled hide
flopped over a crone's skeleton in a
nursing-home bed?

This time, the whole family
huddles in, demanding attention,
ignoring your remains as if you were
already dead.

How can I comfort you, Mother,
with all these others and why
are they here? To scavenge?
Your eyes are all that remain.

Wake up – this dream is a mess.
Tomorrow night I'll start afresh;
we'll be together, alone.
I'll stroke your grey hair, hold your hand.

Still life

At the southern edge of the Red Centre
the Gawler Ranges fringe hot desert.
Granite columns oversee narrow gorges:
sentinels of ferruginous quartzite
they balance, knee-deep in spinifex
giddy from aeons of sun worship.
Some, done with twistings and turnings,
kneel or lie broken; rust into desert.

At Circular Quay, cool as sea-breeze
solemn granite-grey pylons stand:
immutable ghosts of black fishermen
they stretch harbour-wide nets to catch
teeming lights and the rust of sunset.
Painted statues imperceptibly rotate:
the golden lady, the silver man
ignore digital didgeridooers, other buskers,
staring tourists, busy workers,
tooting ferries, the gaiety and the ghosts.
They're dreaming desert-red pillars.

Reconciliation Day

We march the bridge from north to south;
side by side, one day, one voice.

Our statesmen, egos mightier still
than granite pylons, beams of steel,

ignore the mob, reject our calls;
all three-hundred-thousand of us.

Thereby the gap remains unbridged;
the black the white, the poor the rich.

Now nations gather in Sydney
for the sorry olympic corroboree.

And Freeman lights that ancient flame.
She wins her race, her race…

Her race enslaved by lies. What's gained
by flames illuminating games?

Old place harbour; many thousand years
the sandstone waits. Light a candle, dream

of races marooned along these shores
and proud cultures that gently amix.

Fogged in on the Bridge

for Paul in admiration for the genius of his painting

this is me escaping
in a blear of watery colour
on a brush-stroke that's a pushbike
on the slippery road I've made

north across the harbour where the air's
so dense it traps me and
the Quay is quiet with ferries
chafing chains that keep them still

here and there emerging from the murk
are bars of superstructure
verticals that hem me
and remind me of the cells

God! but I will peddle through the damp chill
to the beating of the train
along its tracks to Milsons Point
and then away

Kosciuszko

for Steve

An alpine meadow and you
dozy in late summer sun
ignoring the hint of zephyrs.
They chill and stir everlasting daisies
that won't.
A giant slater iridescent green
is lost in tussocks of fine grasses.
Sphagnum moss surrounds tarns
reflecting really blue sky.
Standing by, granite stacks reach up:
the giants' cairns,
some bygone glacier's playthings,
strewn on an ancient land
worn smooth during the Pleistocene.
Look down at ridge lines:
snow gums now ghost gums
their skeletons in supplication
raising ashen limbs to the heavens.
Centuries of woody growth
killed off by fire after lightning storms
but now resprouting from below the ground
coarse stems with bronzed green leaves.
Rills once home of corroboree frogs
can be followed down without a trace
of their black and yellow stripes.
More chance of chasing down a glimpse
of circean water nymphs in icy pools.
Idyll for now.
Tonight, early snowstorms
will dust all to the same white.

In search of the dreaming colour

1

the primeval urge to climb
get away
view the distant horizon in solitude

there is fascination
for what lies beyond
and the need to be alone

to view the world
on one's own terms

2

You climb against their wishes;
see only roads dividing red earth around Uluru.
Go away!

You stand on the North Rim and strain to see the Grand Canyon
down through the tourists and yellow haze.
Move on.

You queue to do the London Eye and eye khaki sky;
look at topless red buses on black macadam.
Move on.

You step from yak-herder's hut onto the frozen khaki earth.
Glance up at white peaks, clear air.
Go home.

The Nullarbor is bluebush, blue sky and you're there.

Edge trilogy

for Finn

1 *the edge*

loosened
mind wandering
escarpment wilderness
threatening or comforting you
wonder

2 *black*

The space is too big,
the mind loses itself
in this wilderness.
Sheer cliffs
reach up to phobias
on the stony plateau;
in the gorge below
cushioning tree-tops beckon;
a stormy darkness
spreads from the horizon.
Bring plain windowless walls
and dangling naked,
one shining light-bulb;
bring a safety fence,
a spirit in a bottle:
this escarpment is too dangerous
for a wandering mind.

3 *and white*

The space is so big
the mind loosens
in this wilderness.
The gorge echoes with thunder
and a cleft in the cliff invites;
below there is shelter.
No need for walls
safety fence or bottle:
this place is never too dangerous
for a wondering soul
with a mind to wander.

Scarlet's waltz

She is losing the point of her dream in which red was a colour that sauntered. It's something to do with her need to be part of the scene she is painting. The rush of good feelings she gets when she's leaving the place she calls home. Like she's crawled out from under the tedium. Wasn't just dreaming a list. No! A single coherence, her story, a wholeness. Awake now, refreshed and alone in a queen bed. And if she lies still, she is warm but for angular bits as they poke at the quilt where it's threadbare. Her thoughts are as many as trucks on this highway. And each rumbles through like her memory of lovers that pass in the night. In this mean little motel; the outskirts of Dulltown. A rooster is blurting obscenities, though it's still dark. All she wants is to be on the road again, heading way out. But a truck going by's a reminder of hazardous wildlife. Crepuscular urges are drawing the creatures to spring from the verge where they smash into vehicles and die in the dawn. The reverse in the city. The images over and over on telly. The crash of a school bus; with children laid scattered and bloodied all strewn by the kerb. 'If I lived in the desert,' she whispers, 'I'd drive to the mountains and paint ferns in rainforests. And if I lived in the forest, away I would run to the sea. I could not run away to a city, I'm trapped in one – never have wanted to paint cityscapes.' Her escape is a thousand mile drive to the desert. The city just presses, depresses; the people all shove, push and hurry, the air is so grimy with their expectations. As well, even worse, 'are my own expectations! Oppressive!' Embarrassed to hear her voice raised.

Her existence becomes tug o' war between needing to pee and the need for security. Scrunching up tighter and watching her body, complete with her flannelette fashion designer pyjamas, unwinding. A line on the desert; her body is tugged back and forwards across it. Alone by the creek bed, from limbs of a giant dead gum tree, erupts unexpected a thousand galahs with their screeches and rose-coloured breasts. It's that moment in time when the rim of a cold sun peeks over the vastness of sand. Then a scorpion, abdomen raised, is observing the contest. But he's in the foreground and seems to be larger than her. Mesmerised, idly swaying his stinger erect. He remembers his purpose and rushes off wildly all full of himself in the pink of his prime. 'There's a man without malice; that's so rare,' she muses. Now wet lips are brushing her neck from the ear to the shoulder. She quivers. He's gentle, she sunburnt all over. 'You look like a lobster,' he tells her and hands her a flowing vermilion cape. She's embroidering fern sprigs (and that part's made up) to distract the black ants with the spidery legs. Oh! The legs are bright-red and they're dragging her close to the edge of a cliff. They'll succeed, she can see, if they lose fascination with ferns in the desert. Though never so quick with her sewing, her mind is now flying her over the gorge in a timely escape on the delicate wings of a cinnabar moth. Only once in the city she did it. Her boss was pathetically droning his, 'sleep with me honey, I'll pay you more money'.

'I'm not very tired,' she'd said and then floated from view, out the door, on the ferry and never went back. Sure, his slap of 'black trash' was predictable. 'What do you mean, Mum? You can't quit your job!' 'Thanks, you're so understanding,' she tells her and hangs up. The daughter's becoming a huge rufous eagle sent flapping to scowl at oblivion. Male crimson chats with their red caps and chests, pirouette on white quartzite. The glint of the rock is impossibly sharp and she falters, brush poised. But the chats have become a brown blur as they flitter towards her. For cleaning her tent there's a feathery duster that she doesn't use. But she'll sit drinking claret at sunset and watch the sky thicken with dust and the gibber stones vainly cast shadows that lengthen then fade away. Sturt's desert rubies she calls them. She reaches the tube of black paint and a fine brush to give them that burnished appearance; uncovering her arm and the cold of it wakes her.

'…mmm where were you, Scarlet?' She squirms and she smiles. 'Away. Miles away.'

Epyllion for Sydney

Stare across at them for long enough and
the verticals (your confirmation of
order, strength, permanence), the verticals
move.
  At first, just one. And it's so slight that
the game of hide-and-seek comes to mind. Left
eye closed and head tilted right at twenty
degrees, align the offending edge, which
is about sixty storeys high and a
kilometre north, with a 'known', like the
brickwork down the balcony wall. (For now,
your confidence in home is unshaken.)
The lines are *not* parallel. The amount
of tilt can be approximated by
counting squares on transparent graph paper
imagined (you need coffee), imagined…
No! It's real. One edge is bending. This is
not tilt, it's wilt. The XYZ Building
needs coffee.
    Go inside, pour, sip, sigh then
glance surreptitiously at XYZ.
Whew! It's arris edges are restored to
vertical. It was only the eastern
face that sagged: a mini-stroke of concrete
and glass from which it fully recovered.
Wakeful the next morning before sunrise,
pre-coffee, as XYZ tilts then sags
slightly east (just the top ten storeys), you
wonder: do buildings hum Lauds? Balcony-
brickwork hints that XYZ+1 (a

mere twenty-five storeys) is more bowing
than sagging.
          This morning, the coffee pot
corroborates that building construction
has halted as far as the eye can see.
Nine buildings, all near to XYZ, are
deconstructing themselves. Drink your whiskey
from a cup.
        Along the horizon, first
windows then walls are evaporating.
The place is beginning to resemble
grand-scale diablerie.
                 Now it's Thursday.
Sunrise glints off just a few windows but
mostly stares into glassless cavities.
With pot, coffee cup and bottles (water
and whiskey), talk to your bricks. Don't ask for
answers just because the currawongs were
blathering in the plane trees yesterday
about Pisa and Eiffel. Google had
information on 'Invitatory
Psalms' but it's too late for that now. The last
of the yappy dogs was heard this morning
as the city's parasite-load begins
to reduce.
        You begin a list: MISSING:
The noise of dogs, currawongs, police sirens.
Tea and coffee (but that gets scribbled out).
Boiling water, and come to think of it,

tap water because there will be no more
long hot showers, steamy baths, tap water.
Electricity, music, noise, buses,
trucks and cars.
     XYZ and Co. are bent
skeletons now. Plasticity was less
of an issue with those 'sky scrapers' (you
don't hear that expression much these days) north
of the harbour but their skeletal forms
lean on the sky. The harbour, that's it! The
buildings all want to copy the Bridge! HA!!
But meanwhile, the air is solid with a
vapour of concrete and glass.
         Two items
seem to be surviving OK (were you
going to say: 'cockroaches and what?'). Wrong:
it's the ibis and the wheelie-bins. The
cockroaches are all eaten. Earlier,
hateful ibis were seen snatching them from
the last of the cats. Did the buildings' stench
drive the cats off? Ibis forage inside
carcasses, perching on the reo mesh
and steel superstructure. The wheelie-bins,
their primary-coloured carapaces
licked clean, congregate at street corners.
           You
think it odd: in all this silence, none of
the bent or leaning structures has fallen.

Tripping with an angel

In memory of Louise Megaloconomos – your art enriches my life

Here, you've enclosed white spaces.
The black lines tease me to trace
smiling eyes, curve of thighs
and lithesome arms, an outstretched invitation.
The snowflakes and shards of ice
could be bits of me or your charcoal
adding some Euclidean tensions.

Now we're woven into a storm.
Me the thick threads of distant horizons,
tightropes marching down the walls.
You the staccato thunder
pulsing moods vertically
from your cloud to my room.

Wait! Is that you
below my happy perch?
Me, an avian paint blob,
tweeting cheery and innocent song.
Your luscious cat's whiskers
painted into broadest smile
because you are going to eat me.

And here, I feel
the playful ensanguined tentacles
and delicious ruby lips.
I'm victim of mermaids with pert breasts;
fleshy pink with crimson tips.
Lightning startles the sky
as your nets drag me willingly
into waves of red and green and blue
to drown in your rainbow ocean.

But the trip isn't always psychedelic.
You force my gaze through this
not-so-bright window, which frames a wall
whose sombre grime and sneering pipes
I view with a grimace,
while you laugh at suburbia
and my bleak outlook.

Your sparkle touches me every day
but you were never my drug.
Your generous brushstrokes
and excess nervous energy
mark your journey, not mine.
Leave me now, if you must. Go
into your white world
with angel wings. But you can't fly away.
You are trapped with me here at my place.
In acrylic on a parchment shore
we are specs of sand, you and I;
coils on shells, claws on crabs,
algal strands intertwined.
Steady tidemarks
in each others' lives.

From the watchtower

there's tension here
as electrifying as the fences
groupings with tidal wave forces
freshwater and saltwater

surges of them in uniform green
buffet into everything
reverberate with injustices
then swirl apart all the more aggrieved

their scars and deep-held stories
growled in close-lipped dialects
surface briefly
like pleas from the drowning

but there's hope here too
some dark green waves
that were trapped and smashed
have reformed into the story of

a counter-current slipping away
from the push and pull of tide
away from the steel cages
out to the open sea

On lost children

Daughter

Here, you're fixed in this sunset's golden glow;
eyes hinting a smile. My four-year-old child
in the photo from forty years ago.

And now, amber light streams in the window
from thundery clouds. The weather is wild
but you're fixed in the sunset's golden glow.

Remember? Mascara, blush, eye-shadow,
lipstick and the fuss to have your hair styled
for that photo so many years ago.

You're always here for a chat. But you know,
it's unnatural to outlive one's child.
Here, you're fixed in this sunset's golden glow

and a parent's comprehension like slow
anger drains the glass. But you're always mild
in the photo from forty years ago.

Whiskey tears and thirty years of sorrow
well in me. Although, earlier you smiled
there, transfixed in the sunset's golden glow,
in the photo from all those years ago.

Missing boy

for Eliachim Muteba 24 January 2012

You didn't mean to bring media attention
black, refugee, name withheld.
Spectators, their own eight-year-olds
safe on the shore, look on with shaking heads
and begin to comprehend a shattered family's grief.

The air is gasped by helicopters
and jet skis rasping on the choppy surface.
You elude them, deep in an undercurrent of silence
a gentle swirling world where you hide
from the agonies of those you've left.

At first, the surfers respect your solitude
but slowly they return to float above you.
Take company, if you will, from their wave-catching.
Come out of hiding, you could float like them.
Bring your spirit with you.

Helicopter

We met at red DON'T WALK corner
You point and cry in hopeless hope
'Cop-der, cop-der' and Swahili
'They will find him, they will find him'
Your son who drowned nearby last year.
Black refugee you now walk free
I'm wheelchair bound, with hot white tears
Above, the clatter screams our fears.

We grasp each other's shoulders, eyes
Congolese smile for ex-soldier
Your broken teeth, my flaccid legs.
'Helicopter! Vietnam! War!'
I urge, gulping noise-shattered air.
Sensing each other's worst terror
Is the only comfort we share
Green WALK back to private nightmares.

Gaunt epigones

From the moment they begin to toddle
you begin to lose.
With their every stutter, stumble, tumble
they take control.

The truth about them is what
scares you most: the monsters
that you imagine are created
in your image.

Sleepless trauma of your making:
alone you agonise, apologise
confront their demons, debts, misfortunes;
pay your penance,

make amends, take on guilt, self-blame,
fail – and they care?
No.
    Just wish them well, sweetness.
Their thanks will never haunt you.

Giving up light

Oh! The cat had kittens	Thus, you give stuff away
And that's that	Shunt responsibilities
Work doesn't suit everyone	There goes your career
We weren't compatible, I guess	As you renounce loved ones and
Well stuff them anyway	Who needs family?
Promises: I give them away	You can never keep them
Think of it as early retirement	But you had so much more to give
Getting up in the mornings?	I know it's tough for you
Unlikely; I'm zoned out	Are you surrendering hope?
Suicide's an option	Or hanging a threat over us
If I can be bothered	Remembering, your laugh still lights the room

Song from Keleni

Where is that voice calling
me back to life
from this lonely abyss
in the dead of the night?
I am scared in this silence
come quickly I need you.

Here is your voice again
soft, low and humming
the pulse of your words
I imagine you're with me
you're whispering strength to me
calling me calming me.

Where is the hand that held
mine when I needed it?
Stroking me pulling me
back from the edge
of this terrible nightmare
hold tightly I need you.

Here is your hand again
warm reassuring
I dream it is touching me
strumming a song and
that voice singing on to me
calling me soothing me.

You can't always be here
for my needs and my heart stops.
Remember I wanted your
hum and your song and
your hands to safeguard me.
    And now Dad, I'm gone.

On the bright side

that kind of rainy indoors day
when the cat curls on the hearth
the ghost of a girl plays piano
dreamily: *Moonlight Sonata*, *Clair de lune*
a friend calls to say the weather's clearing
then that good book calls from the fireside

that kind of sunny city day
when people are friendly
the old buildings are more than facades
you enter a holy place for solace
light a candle for a boy and his Lego
and leave teary but glad

no need for conversation, reincarnation
the dog stretches full-length, yawns flops and settles
a grandchild is nodding and smiling
the Buddha within seems optimistic
and that's it: the celerity of a lifetime spent well
it's been that kind of day

On trains and the occasional bus and ferry

The Ghan

From the Ghan you stare at me
The wheels clunk slowly through our town
You're the one I always see
The well-dressed bloke who's looking down

Tuesdays when the train comes through
The whole town stops beside the track
Often there's not much to do
You stare at me because I'm black

One by one we drift away
To favourite shady trees again
You've seen The Alice, so you stay
In air-con comfort on the train

Tuesday next the train comes through
There'll be another man like you
Glaring down because I'm black
The Ghan will take him down the track

Tourist haikus en route to Yellow Water river cruise

Tommy sees nothing
Why bus me through this
land emptied of green and call
it world heritage?

Sam sees colours
From zilch but red land
to river green. Crocodile!
Guys! Open ya eyes!

Koko sees all
Easy river shade
after bustling hot desert.
Kakadu teems life.

Watching him, watching them

As MV *Freshwater* leaves the Quay
Smart phones snapping
Tourists' faces with backdrops
Harbour Bridge, Opera House
For Instagrams sent off
Then on-line shopping for more fashion wear

The Heads roll past
Spraying unsuspecting Facebookers
Kids race about squeaking
Grandparents scuttle to grab at little hands
Serious-wearers smooth their creaseless suits

Disembarking
Pensioners to Manly RSL where there's food 'to die for'
Thighless blokes in shorts with the brickies' cleavage
Laugh with girls showing legs that go right up
Their cheeky bums peeking out from tattered denim
Show illicit tattoos

His knowing smile
Reflected back at me

Whazisname from the commuters' club

Remember he used to sit there by the window
The old bloke reserved as he stared out to sea.
With self-conscious chuckle he'd scratch at the crossword
The afternoon cryptic, he once said to me.

Apparently he was a big boss in Sydney
His morning routine was a book and some fruit.
A government job we supposed or a banker
High-class evident from his poise and his suit.

On Sunday I saw him all bearded and shaggy
He strode from the surf looking forty again.
I nodded polite thinking he wouldn't know me
All smiles he asked keenly, Mate! how goes the train?

Orienteering in the suburbs

Be prepared, I cogitate
in the vestibule. It amuses me to live
the old-school adage, standing ready
to depart my air-con carriage at Sutherland.

She rises from her seat on the platform
without lifting her eyes. Her sense
of the arriving train fascinates me. I remain; just
an old dork, stepping back while she daze-walks

towards the slide of opening doors.
She's been to all the stores, parcels hooked
and dangling from her crooked left arm;
right palm cradles her reality, the banality

of her life tapped by thumb on iPhone. From
elsewhere her numb eyes suck images.
Beep, beep, beep, the doors slide closed with her face
agape, reflected in departing windows.

The rest of her on the platform still.
My brain ajangle, thinking: where do I get out?
Dill! I shout. In my hand, car keys jingle. And…yes.
Today I drove to Sutherland.

The train home

A welty-faced woman,
'Arse ya fa da.
Ya shouldent evun be ere;
go arkse ya fa da.'
A quiet minute of train beat:
Curdung-curdunk, curdung-curdunk…

'You shuddup.
Whaddah ya cry yen for?
Git orf me foot.
Ah shuddup, Ryan.'
Backyards rush by.
Curdung-curdunk, curdung-curdunk…

Graffitied walls,
parked cars, bricks, tiles and
tribes of tall posts
strung together in silence.
Curdung-curdunk, curdung-curdunk…

Ryan ain't dumb.
He ain't gunna say what he thinks:
You're the only one talking, so
Shut! Up! Mum!
The heat is oppressive.
Curdung-curdunk, curdung-curdunk…

Suburban stops
for other families.
'Geddoudovit!' with which
the four-year-old gets
a whack across the ear.
'Aww Ma-a-um.'
'Awh nothin.
Far korf and shud! your! mouth!'
Ryan knows his little sister
has wet herself.
Curdung-curdunk, curdung-curdunk…

Brightly:
'Our stop, Mum.'
And Ryan, holding the little one's hand,
leads his four sibs along the platform.
The train heads off:
Curdung-curdunk, curdung-curdunk…

The bloke at the station

'It doesn't go right through then?'

Can't read, 'ad ta ask this bloke.
'e looks a bit rough but 'e says
to change at Wollongong,
wait fer the express ta Sydney.

Sometimes, people move away from me.

'I'm goin' up to see this girl in re-'ab.'
'e nods. 'She's a user.
First 'usband ODed. Ya know what I mean?'
'e says straight:

people dyin' a drugs is bad.

'She's been done fer drink drivin' again.
That's why she's put 'erself into re-'ab.
Tryin' to make 'erself look good
so they won't send 'er to jail.'

'e nods.

'She says she, like,
loves me!
But I know she can't;
she can't jus' say that.'

'She can't mean it, can she?'

'Like, she's only sayin' it 'cause
I'm the only one what visits 'er.'
The bloke says I wanta be careful.
I don't say 'er name cause

sayin' it upsets me.

'e's like me, this bloke:
the baseball cap, grey beard,
flanno shirt, el cheapo sandshoes
but when 'e smiles,

'is face crinkles, like.

'No one'll talk to 'er.
Mother, daughter, no one. Jus' me.
Maybe she's usin' me.'
We agree on that.

I finish off me breakfast burger and

'ere comes the train.
'e smiles and puts 'is 'and on me shoulder.
All the best mate, 'e says.
'Yeah, thanks mate. See ya.'

White Christmas on Route 184

from inside our bus
we feel the hush of snow
there's no puff of exhaust smoke
from the line of traffic ahead
we breathed the last of it
from the recycling truck
seems like weeks ago
we saw the garbage workers
abandon truck at the blockage
hopefully they're safe inside a pub

it began as storms do with
a swirling flurry and
a string of brake lights
in the bleary dusk
down the hill
they tried to back up
but that was going nowhere

our FirstGroup driver is
slumped and snoring in uniform
we're still here gazing at
rooftops of snowed-in cars
and an awning advertisement at the
Peasedown St John Veterinary Surgery
proclaiming
    December Offer
Your once-loved pets consigned to rest with dignity

how wonderfully comforting and Christmassy
but will they extend the offer
to us on the bus?

Ballad of solicitation

Her skin was smooth, deliciously so
her eyes were sparkling green
her wavy hair was orange-gold
her smile the sweetest seen.

She singled me out on a crowded train
she gazed, she swooned, she eyed
she had a salacious lilt to her voice
she tilted her head and enquired.

I heard her words in a fuddled haze
I felt for my Seniors' Card
I wondered what she saw in me
I yearned with an old fool's heart.

Her meaning came slowly sinking in
oh yes, she was heavenly sent
with filial respect she was offering her seat
to an ageing grey-haired gent.

On love

Natural selection

if only it was that easy
to explain
your glance
our first five minutes
the next fifty years
of romance

Oyster Bay

for my love, 14 February

Cuts on your hands and knees
from oyster shells
that dot the intertidal.

The moss is slippery green.
Also, frilly lichens:
one turquoise, another luminescent lime
together on the trunk
of a sprawling fig tree
slumped down like you
at the edge of the bay.

But the morning belongs to the rocks
with their hues and patterns:
fine vertical stripes of dark chocolate
in a matrix of cream,
cake-sized pebbles in yellow walls
with coffee swirls,
honeycombing in honey-coloured sandstone
splashed with a dusky pink
warmer, more vibrant than blood.

Demented unconformities of geomorphology:
lines that come and go
like phone reception,
delicious stratigraphic stories
on every boulder and old rock face.

What? You're bleeding?
Oh sorry!
No mobile cover.
You'll just have to die here
on this gorgeous Hawkesbury shoreline.

Moonlight and adults tarry

their touch, their lust illegal in the night
was born of loneliness and wanton flight
a kindred hope: some momentary spark
might ease their spirits' angst, their empty hearts

a whispered song became a desperate dance
despite the risks their yearning was intense
the icy water beckoned and they swam
what consequence, who's hurt – who gives a damn

how violently they trembled, frenzied hands
that tore away at flesh; by what command
a unity of soul ascended there
then fell in private shackles of despair

'twas long ago and yet one memory's near
the moon was up, the lake was shining clear*

* line 85/468 from Book 1 of *The Two-book Prelude*, Wordsworth 1798–9

The kiss

for Kira

first kiss just being polite
or a teasing pleasure in the night?
footpath mingling dance-floor
with the watchers and waltzers
and the flashing bright lights
jostling with movie buffs
queued for virtual excitement
and sated lovers spilling from
drink-loudened restaurants

a sign flashes 'don't walk'
and the dance is suspended
statues stand at dance-floor corners
like that game when the music stops
then a tram rattles past
the city-street music
        continues to play
in slow pirouette she beckons

second kiss extends the pleasure
the tease and the tension
'don't dance' signs flash
imagine prohibited steps
wild rock 'n' roll
seductive Latin-American

third kiss – that breathless song
of inevitability
toe to twitching toe
eye to lustful eye –
the third kiss is denied

Fantasia

beyond the wine-blurred edges
where it's all been said and done
the soothing words already spoken
smiles and confidences exchanged
of dalliances real and imagined…
there's the desperate need to be held

so they strip down to the youths that they were
then glancing into mirrors askance
quickly redress in the years they own
sip more red wine, muse privately
play familiar tunes, softly say 'goodnight'
they know about tomorrows and regrets

The fifteen-year rule

Sharing unspoken words. Comfortable,
their arms brush as they reach
across the lunch table for food
and a quiet reassurance that mad
is not her preferred option. She is
newly 'separated' and her
fragments are jagged. But in this
company, she feels the urge to smile.

Glimpsing possibilities beyond the window,
eyes squeezing out the glare, she laughs out loud
so as not to be thought of as whispering.
Daily she rebuilds; gains confidence and
respect for the reserve of this liaison.
He has a child her age.

A rose

another long-stemmed rose, a bud
like the threat of a clenched fist

waved in her face
like a dare to object

a sign flashing red
like she must not move

from the bloodied thorn
like staying is self-abuse

each day, a knife to shorten the stem
like paring back helps her to forget

denial, except for dream words
like cut, leave

but the threat returns
like the gift of a rose

With what's left

After a long illness – the symptoms of
which were unnoticed by me – our love died.
Was it so cryptic or just me wanting
not to know about your changing patterns?
You've explained it all to me now, that you
hated this and that with me. For decades!
And you've developed this new friendship. Well
that's reason enough to leave me, you say.

A person from our former circle tells
that you've always had other special friends.
Anyone among them that I knew? No!
Don't smash me with any more of your truths.
My hate for you runs deeply; all the way
to my lawyer. You won't get a penny.

Love again

for Rayma and Ross, 20 December 2014

There was debris everywhere:
imploding and exploding universes
and only the fittest survived.
Minds travelling easily,
souls living dangerous,
hearts taking chances.

In a moment of metaphoric chaos
your paths crossed.
The separate journeys to that point
are your histories: very interesting but
not the foundations of the moment
and not a guide to the future.

With carefree distraction
you'll each wander alone.
Alone but never lonely.
And the favourite new-trod paths you share,
your place, your peace, your intimate affair;
to have a mate,
all this is answer to your common prayer.

Moondancer

14 February

You swing on your mooring
waltz on the tide
rumba in the wake
of the faster boats
rock and roll on the swell
as we motor past the heads.

You float in a dream
quiver on a crest
at my lightest touch
moonbeams and this
is as close as you'll get
to the tango fully naked.

Yo ho, the two-step
we were holiday sailors
on our little houseboat.

To be left on the shelf

although the raw material varies
the temporal pleasures are the same
with each affair
desire first, always
possibilities eyed, hands twitch
then the scent
and peeling off layers
to discover secrets
a twist, a sound; the flaws, the gifts
and if we care and we're gentle
we'll bring new life to the world
'wood' is such a plain word
'piece of wood' belies, denies
each time, the inscrutable allure

Random stuff

A short history of animals

The earth cools
a crust solidifies
pushes pulls buckles
heats distorts cracks
glaciers come and go
thunderous rivers
pummel shards
smoothing edges

On one such pebble
a Buddhist paints
animals cooperating
elephant monkey rabbit bird

One last blink
they're all extinct

Air

it's not enough to know it's there
it takes your thanks and hopes in prayer
sent to what? but does it matter?
as long as you can have a chatter
in this friendly medium
don't pray to god because she, um…
she's busy starting off new wars
and drafting anti-carbon laws
so treat your senses to the air
tomorrow it might not be there

In the Simpson Desert

for my friend, Dr Janet Cohn

Despite the severity, the inevitability
of death from life,
the balance seems
fair enough in the desert.

Life is mostly harsh light
but the shade at dawn is exquisite
and twilight can be civil indeed.
The pace is attuned to time at a stand still:
sand dunes overlook forever,
silence is punctuated by singular bird calls,
spinifex and canegrass whisper their songs,
cursorial creatures foot-print their stories in scurries;
the periodicity of boom and bust
has the familiarity of a long-lost friend.

From a stony rise
thought is open,
unconstrained by trees,
without secrets. But the history
of this place is mostly unknown:
there's detail to discover in the flatness
and buried beneath the sand-drifts.

Stars crowd in on moonless nights
and tears gleam back at them
grateful for the solitude.
Knowing elsewhere,
makes this place special.

Blocked images from 1588

for Jordy

The government gives me a laptop then school blocks me accessing stuff on
the internet. How can I do any homework? They've disabled Google!
I have to have photos. The Spanish Armada (God! history is so wrong)
is due in tomorrow. The system is dumb. I'll just frigginwell doodle

and dream about how I will spend all the wages I'm earning at Woollies.
… I'll rage at a concert or chill over coffee or hang at the movies…
'Medina Sidonia had no instamatic!' says Grandpa. He's fully
just bull-shitting. What about wiki? There's Twitter. And Facebook's got selfies.

Cynical exercise

for Tony

the morning gym class in the park
talks loss of weight and faith in politics
they play lack-lustre with a huge truck tyre
taking turns to roll it forth and back
like a Bill shuffled between the Houses
and when it's amended beyond use
they lift and flop it end over end

they're with Team Australia
jumping into and out of the hole
like the trained guerrilla but overall
they've got PMs and tyres to spare

Frescos revealed

Inspired by poems from *Rain and Hirohito* by Barbara Fisher

We begin with radiant child on Mother's lap.
They're painted as usual:
this one of many virgins is so voluptuous.
Seated and shedding the scratchy pastoral gloom
her breasts stare out at us
wearing nothing but modesty.
His miraculous pelt is uncovered:
rounded tummy and bottom escape from swaddle,
a divine willie peeking at lifelong abstinence.
We stifle our mischief and read the brochure
like a huddle of cherubs in prayer.

Huntsman's sea change

Inverted eight-legged limpet clings
to walls and ceiling. Unnoticed
it huddles flat behind seascape.
Nymphs, crabs, starfish and gastropod
stare through the glass of cobwebbed frame
above the mantle piece. The coast
seems clear and with this limpid view
their arachnophobias ease.

In three steps

                  one two three   a slow pace
                    left right left   in the Himalayas
                  slow slow slow   like steps in a dream
                        in a dream   breath out two three
   living one breath at a time   in two three
   the exertion is mechanical   the challenge is all in the mind
          way above the treeline   timeless scenery is a distraction
      altitude sickness threatens   at five thousand metres
               slow slow slow then   the summit
     at last you can see forever   and there, is your spirit

Petrified wood

…the shard of a tree
that split from the trunk
that flew from the lightning
that sank in the mire
that soaked up the earth
that fused with some pebbles
that cooked and distorted
that hardened like axe heads
that time had abandoned
that washed and eroded
that swashed on the seashore
that charmed the old lapidary
that made a stone pendant
that shone with new life

Janet

in memory of Janet Cosh 1901–1989

Your sweet gifts of waratah. The sketches
paintings. Artful pressings of wildflowers
serene in their youthful blossom like you
    in that photo.

Born in the year of Federation
white Australian, like a pale English rose
demure only child. Your father thought you
too delicate for maths. So you studied
    Greek and Latin.

And you were perennial. You naturalised
exchanging lace for sensible outdoor wear.
With your women friends, in a battered ute
on back roads, you relaxed into the seasons
learning your country, searching and finding
    floral treasures.

Like an indigenous rock artist you
painted over the canvas of your forebear
covering his stale landscapes with your life
    a bloodline ends.

Your pencil and brush have captured the hues
of *Boronia* and *Dampiera*
the golden wattle and *Dillwynia*
spidery scarlet of *Telopea*.
Telopea indeed! Tell of hope here:
For while you were childless your gifts have spawned
new generations of botanisers
    in your image.

for the launch of *Flowering Wonderfully: The Botanical Legacy of Janet Cosh* 2012

Jhomolhari spirit

April 2011 at Jangothang base camp, 4,080 metres

At Jangothang in early spring
there's heavy snowing for an hour.
Your thunder drowns
the clatter of the Paro Chhu
washing boulders in its riverbed.
Close by, their bells on red ribbons,
stand the yaks.
Marmots hide in their burrows.
Himalayan griffon float away
to quieter valleys.

An hour before sunset
you brood under cloud
taking with you your glaciers
and the threat of avalanche.
Our tiny orange dome tents poke through
white powder, the ponies shiver and
stop their search for green pickings.

Two hours later,
draped in moonlight,
your silhouette rises
beyond the rounded valley
carved over the Ice Ages.
You glare down on the ruin
of the Dzong built mere centuries ago
as shelter from your storms
and Tibetan enemies.

The Dzong whispers confidences.
You stand back in a frozen silence.
Momentarily, a vast cloudless dawn
has equalled your spirit.

Jhomolhari, 7,314 metres – one of the high peaks in the Kingdom of Bhutan

Pop's fob watch

for Star

Your World War II issue
Omega pocket watch
still works.
It fits into the palm
of my granddaughter
firm and comfortable
as the memory
of your handshake.
She is fascinated
that it has no batteries.
It winds her up!

Silence

The brush of a zephyr stirs spinifex,
on starlit tracks busy rodents scamper,
neighbourly howling from distant dingoes
and a spotted nightjar's weird *cook ook ook*.
Ubiquitous buzz of unknown insects,
the sharp crack of car-metal contracting.
Miles above, jet mumblings taper away.
The campfire hesitates, hisses and glows.

Between sounds, anticipation expands
comfortably into night. It's freezing
but there's no threat in the darkness. Each pulse
of calm brings reverence for the wilderness.
The brush of your hand says we can suspend
breathing, listen to our lust, sit and wait.

Shadow racer

The crunch of boots on gravelly road,
a gibber kicked aside,
the thud of kangas bounding off.
A gentle pace? I lied.

A shadow chased me up the road
then raced me right back home.
We hit the ruts, they shook us good
they rattled out this pome.

Footsteps pounding east to dawn,
the breathing's hard and deep.
A rhythm and nobody's singing along.
The birds? Mate, they're still asleep.

A shadow…

Up bobs the sun, it's time for a pause
now you've caught up to me.
I shoot a glance at those silly long legs
but you've already turned to flee.

A shadow…

The game is on and it's westward now
striding out with your one two three.
Time's short'ning your legs and I've hatched a plan:
cunning, you'll see.

A shadow…

As we round to the south I'm up the inside
with a burst of acceleration,
you're trapped out wide, I've got you caught
in the worst of the road's corrugations.

A shadow…

We're neck and neck, you're hopeful still
as I slow to a walk and a laugh.
In through the gate and you're well behind
going east up the garden path.

A shadow chased me up the road
then raced me right back home.
We hit the ruts, they shook us good
they rattled out this pome.

Saturday morning is all right

Rushing in the traffic. On the hands-free going, *don't start without us*
Wondering if I look smart enough and it's like, *MUM! MUM!*
Blaring at me, this huge red sign, *WRONG WAY GO BACK*

OH MY GOD! Execute an emergency U-turn. Swear under my breath
Oops, I say out loud to the twins. How I hate foul language
They'll probably think of a bribe after the game but that's OK

Taylor! Get on the wing! Get on the wing! I yell at my girl's two ears
Supported by the coach, *spread out, spread out guys* (meaning girls and boys)
But what do adults know about the on-field workings of mixed under-8s soccer?

Bees swarming. Ten red (them) and ten blue (us). *KICK IT! KICK IT!*
Squeal (for girls). Squeak (for boys). My Adam yelling, *pass to me, to me, to mee!*
At each end, their goals abandoned (like bored lovers), #11s chat with passers-by

The ball is forsaken when a puppy, a Border collie, joins the game
There's chasings until it's caught and escorted from the field
With a red and blue guard of honour; all the players cheering and patting

Then it's, *back in your goal, back in your goal.* (there's two #11s)
#4 blue is carried off. *He's only winded!* #7 red is doing fairy bounces, arms by side
Eyes closed, back turned. *Tamara! Tamara! The ball! The ball!*

My device buzzes and I chat with Bruce for ages; really nice and keen as
I wonder about Mum and text her but she's unreliable with the mobile
Not a biggie. We'll drop in on the way home. Maybe she'll have the kids overnight

Pass to me, to me, to mee! And a confused red player kicks to Adam
He's played a strong game without actually touching the ball until now
And so, in this scoreless game, my boy rockets towards the goal

He drives the ball home to a chorus of, *Wrong way, Adam! Wrong way! TWEE-TWEE-TWEEAWEET!* And it's, *three cheers for the Ref! RA! RA! RA!* In the car, *please can we get a puppy? Please Mummy. Can we?*

Maybe. We'll talk to Grandma about it.
Yeah! Yeah! We can! We can!
MAYBE, I said. All right? ALL RIGHT!

The quoll song

From dawn to dusk, a whiff of musk is all you know of me.
By night I prowl, I hiss and growl and I sneak to get me tea.
Me tail is long and me ears are cute
there's big cream spots on me golden suit
and chicken giblets are me favourite fruit.
I'm a quoll, a quoll

White Leghorns then a bantam hen is my idea of heaven.
Rhode Island Reds or broiler's heads. Oh! Once I ate eleven.
I favour fowl play and please note
I once dined out on Australorp
and I cocked-up bad when he stuck in me throat.
I'm a quoll, a quoll

So you will hear me loud and clear it's chooks that make me drool.
I love their names but wait, what games are you playing out of school?
Nomenclature is set by law.
Your names for me stick in my craw.
I'll tell you once and I'll tell you o'er.
I'm a quoll, a quoll

I'm not a pussy, not a cat
nor a curled up tabby by the fireside mat
I'm not a moggy and that is that.
I'm a quoll, a quoll

A tiger quoll I'm not at all. Nor a native cat, you dill.
I'm a proud as hell marsupial, six teats and a pouch as well.
I claw and bite when I'm in a fight.
If you get bitten I don't give a shite.
I've got a name so get it right.
I'm a quoll, a quoll

Wombat, bilby, kangaroo
possum and koala too
marsupials all through and through
like the quoll, a quoll

That's all from me. Zoology, can get a little boring.
Enjoy your chicken fricassee, I'm back to my chook gnawing.
You and monkeys are placental
you've got no pouch, it's elemental.
I'm marsupial but don't get sentimental.
I'm the vicious spotted-tailed quoll.

A parody of Bernard Bolan's song 'A Gnome' and sung to the same tune.

The girters' anthem

We bound along by edgy girt,
our sandy toes dodge doggy dirt.
Rejoice in knowing concrete pipes
are seaward-sending people's shites.

We gather up the plastic strewn
and carefully avoid the bloom
of algae with its beach-cast smells
and broken glass and smashed-up shells.

We sidestep tide-washed cuttlefish
then gazing wave-ward make a wish
afloat along the girt to be
like gangling surfies young and free.

Beyond, awaiting vacant docks,
are foreign ships that take the rocks;
our tax-free rocks both rich and rare
are nature's gifts for us to share.

For others from across the sea,
regardless of the place you flee,
our fair is not a carnival,
the plains are bounded after all.

Inside our girt is tricky stuff.
Fair maybe just: just not enough.
And even if you're fair of skin
you'll need a magnate next of kin.

We exercise, there's wealth for toil,
join us: the beach is golden soil.
Your joyful strains will not subvert
our courage, jogging by the girt.

postscript
I met an Aborigine
who sang 'Advance, come home with me.
Combine our hearts and hands, White Dross,
our children will be Southern Cross.'

So now when we go girty jogs
with six brown kids in swimming togs,
we pray for them a land of health,
an Aussie fair, a common wealth.

For seniors

A (little) bloke's look

for Jackson

By showing him where it is,
how to search systematically,
how to look with the eyes,
not to look with the voice,
with his, 'I can't find it.'
'It's not there, Grandma.'
'Honest, it's gorne.'
She thinks that she can overcome
aeons of genetic engineering.

It's not cricket

1 *Hairs on it*

A good innings and you've come to understand:
what to love, when to hesitate, how to cope;
that age becomes a barrier, a teacher
from whom you learn 'growing old's got hairs on it.'
They sprout willy-nilly where they choose to grow.
First on ankles then under armpits and yikes!
all around those unmentionable places;
then unfeminine moustaches and for men
grotty bristly blow-flies' legs hang from nostrils.
And worst: the furry-koala-ear syndrome.
One day, a disoriented follicle…

2 *A poke in the eye with a burnt stick*

…sends forth an eye-ward-growing hair; pale and fine,
its feath'ry stroke pressing firmer with each blink
till the full-on lashing sends you moaning to
the optometrist who's an expert plucker.
Instant relief. But in time it regrows and
a fumbling medico breaks the lash. Instant
needle torture. It's then you learn not to blink.
At last, ophthalmologists' green-light laser,
stronger with each visit, deletes the cruel lash.
As the smell of burning hair and flesh recedes,
neuralgia strengthens. Maybe time to pull up
stumps.

Pre-op

Night was all bruised dreams; waking cathartic.
Almost dawn, walking on the beach. As the
air brightens and colours, they turn away
leaving clouds to bleed down the eastern sky,
stain the horizon, fade. Without recourse,
waves pulse onto the sand, spent and confused.
He disturbs purple reflected in pools.
Afraid of an attack by the sea, she stands

well back. The space between them is lightly
tamped by gulls' wings but no eagle soars in
blue sky. They ponder hospitals, rehab,
the waning moon, an afterwards and their
missed opportunities for hand-holding;
the ordinariness of this last day.

Mettle detector

in memory of Uncle Doug

The first time I went through one of those airport contraptions
that really set me off. It was only
my boots but I was thinking shrapnel;
back in Korea lying face down, unable to breathe,
in a forest wondering about death.

Before that, with the occupying forces in Hiroshima,
knowing they started it and dropped a bomb on my brother in Darwin
but I couldn't hate them.
They slid silent along their streets as if
a loud step might bring another bomb on them.
You couldn't look at their skin.
Dad said the army must be a good life *after* a war.
He served in the first and second wars,
which left him strong and no less taciturn but once
I shook the peaceful smile he carried when I told him
it was their eyes: I meant the shock; it was in their eyes.

Thank God the Vietcong went easy on us.
And warrant officers only led a few night patrols.
Those bamboo booby traps were a worry
but there was no excuse for the boys abusing the locals,
for the boozing and the drugs.
And thank God Gough got us out of there.

Dad was right about the good life.
In Papua New Guinea, setting up battalions,
preparing them for independence
was a proud way to finish my thirty years of service.

Thirty years on and I'm wondering
about this coronary rehab place.
Fighting for my life again.

On coiling

A snake is not a garden hose.
With scaly coils tail tip to nose
your average asp quite likes a twist
and waits for food and drink and hist.
A viper warm from sun and blissful
likes to feel well-turned and hiss-full.

Elapids nip with teeth of poison,
hugging is the game of pythons.
Fangs or squeezing – either way –
you wouldn't want to be their prey.

And note that garden hose and snake
must ne'er be struck upon by rake.
The asp will rear and strike at it;
the pressured hose will writhe and spit.
And whereas snakes are pro-constriction,
it would be utter dereliction
to coil a hose and make it bend
and cut the flow to nozzle end.

So don't make your hose a twisted snake:
uncoil and loose it for freedom's sake.
For if you turn around and coil it:
Satin's viper's truth – you'll spoil it.

On composting

A compost bin is not a purse
nor handbag. Yet it is a curse
that all these three get overfilled
with fall-out stuff that spreads and spills
and causes angst to tidy minds
who can't appreciate these finds.

Rarely will a thing of value
fall from purse or bag gone askew.

Unseemly, smelly, foetid plops,
the stuff from compost bins that drops
like crap left by that doorstep duck
(it lost its head for all that muck)
worst spill of all this over cramming.
It should be stopped; it is worth damning.

Whereas your purse or leather bag
accommodates with stretch or sag,
your honest, solid compost bin
is fixed in size. Now that's no sin!
Learn not to fill it to the brim!
And likewise, purse and bag keep slim.
You never know, the space you're saving
may catch a falling star from heaven.
Remember stella's clear sagacity:
Always stay below capacity.

Requited love atop Lady Barrington

At Barrington Tops National Park

With gasping breath and thudding heart we quest
Ignoring pains that stab and doubts that call
Each man with lust for her will do his best
To blaze the trail, to conquer by nightfall.

Our world – each twinge of consciousness – is strapped
And shouldered. Razor sweat on nail-scratched back.
With loin's dull ache, mind numb, our fate is mapped
Each thorn-etched face now trudges up her track.

Our trembling limbs cry out, we breast the peak
Tormented miles of climbing, suddenly done.
Desire quenched, in packs our spirits seek
The walkers raise a glass. The climb was fun.

And have you mused: life's mountains are a spoof?
Then take this earnest sonnet as your proof.

Pre-breakfast snack

You've tossed and turned and fluffed all night
Morning radio's got it right
It's raining so there'll be no walk
We'll stay in bed
        but just to talk
And nothing serious…

We'll hava cuppa reminisce
I'll probably try to steal a kiss
And touch your thigh it's smooth gawd strewth
No wrinkles there
        and that's the truth
All this without me specs…

You could be warming to the task
I feel intention in your grasp
The tea will spill! Well put it up!
Not that you cry
        I meant the cup!
Honestly! At your age…

You're not all sinewy and tough
Crunchy boned and leathery rough
You're creamy warm and freshly baked
Soft butterfly wings
        my plump cupcake
And when I find my teeth…

To remember two

Remember, it takes two to tango
But you need a four-digit code
Which explains why you unlock your mobile with 2514
Ben (second, fifth and fourteenth letters)
Was your first lover
Your ex-husband's birthday 0212
Was a handy number but forget him

Remember, you had a Mother
The year of her birth 1912
That gives you a four-digit PIN
For the credit card
She disapproved of so strongly

Remember the child
Who gives you alphanumeric
Combinations ad nauseam
19Born62; 19Died72
Case-sensitive
But it doesn't bring her back

None of the kids come back

Remember?
You try not to
Although in Lotto
2 is your lucky number
Because B is the second letter
And the only letter common to all their names
You'd like to wish them luck
The living and the dead

You gave them unusual names
Easy for you to remember
Hard for cyber thieves to steal
Easy for them to drift away

The everyday necessity of passwords
Helps you to log on to your memories

Real names and dates have been
Suppressed for security reasons
2 Feb 2002

Tenet of place

for Ron Pretty

our heroes are here before us
flummoxing about
the laws of location are mystifying
and mystified they search
the pages of their poems
yet can't quite find the place
the reasons of place
have slipped from their books

we paid to be in the audience
they're up on the stage
and can't see that
they've earned their place

A farewell hug

In memory of Doug Allen, August 2013

And you were laid up
with half your liver
and the other half chopped out

And I made you laugh
with you begging me not to
and showing off your stitches

And enjoying each other's company
with your prognosis positive
and your optimism as always

And you were glad to be done
with chemotherapy
and said how ill you felt with it

And we sat late one afternoon
with 'how's old what's-'is-name'
and mid-strength beers

And later a bit of red wine
with just a hint of 'the good old days'
and guarding only against hangovers

And another time on the veranda
with morning cuppas
and 'how lucky I've been'

And then the time to say goodbye
with handshakes, tears
and finally, a real blokes' hug

Widow at evensong

In a deep recess of his wild romantic tumult,
the gentle earthliness of Rachmaninoff's *Vespers*.
Air dividing into notes of singular beauty,
voices giving hope and transcending peace.
And yes it's beyond understanding
and yes there are tears;
as often happens in the evening
there are thoughts of her
with her recent title.
And my prayer
    that tomorrow will treat her lightly.

Winter surfer

Stare out from safety beach. A magic spell
a blink. Your mind's adrift, you're there again
with yellow malibu. And Mary Jane
the drug of choice made every ocean swell
a perfect breast. Bikini dreams you know
are safe. Not so wild surfs with crushing waves.
You watch: young men are pumping hard. You gaze.
Their feats'd kill you if you tried, although

you won't. Your feet will paddle, hang about
with seaweed. An old salt; a retiring
beach-cast man with calcified thoughts. Alone,
the sandy swash covers your steps without
a trace. While fresh prints will appear in spring,
you're lost and loneliness is all you own.

Sunset clause

our favourite time and place
the earth preparing to spin the sun away
and the squeeze of your hand says
look! the horizon is reaching up
your eyes follow as my finger traces
the red outline of a ghost cloud
almost touching, touching, then gone

if I spin around
in the dark and cold
on the earth that swallowed you
will you rise up in the morning
or abandon me to the patterns of
darkening colours on distant clouds
the interminable wintery nights

enough of freezing, go indoors
scratch out inutile words
about sharing drinks at sunset
an artist's need for deprivation
that old people want to be touched
and we should have agreed
to go together

Acknowledgements

'Birds move. They fly and perambulate over land; fly over and swim in water. And for millennia...' was the glorious opening of my final scientific publication. I say glorious because of the stunning first sentence, the inclusion of the almost extinct semicolon in the second sentence and the 'And' to start the third sentence; and I say *was* because it got changed in the process of being published. As one of the seven editors and reviewers noted, 'I appreciate the <u>authors</u> attempt at a more poetic scientific language, but...' (my underlining, their omission of apostrophe). Undaunted, I am grateful to the many people who have inspired and encouraged me to be creative with my writing.

My enthusiasm for writing began thirty years ago with Bruce Dawe's *Sometimes Gladness*. It was nurtured through my twenty years of writing science, particularly in association with Rob Whelan, and sustained by reading and rereading great poetry, especially that of C.J. Dennis, W.B. Yeats and Thomas Hardy.

The South Coast Writers Centre has provided me with many opportunities: to participate in monthly meetings of the Poetry Book Club and the Poetry Writers' Group, to be a tutor with the Black Wallaby Writers Group, to publish some of my writing and to attend numerous events.

Dorothy Jones encouraged me with her insightful critiquing of my writing. Catherine Cole, Professor of Creative Writing, University of Wollongong, gave me useful feedback on my writing and confidence in the standard of it. Michael *the sage* Bedward gave detailed critical appraisal of many of my poems (some of which subsequently did not make it to the collection!).

Lizz Murphy provided a professional assessment of an earlier draft of the collection.

Ron Pretty has given a huge amount of his time to mentor the poet in me. When I discovered his textbook *Creating Poetry*, I immediately set about working through it (twice!). Nowadays, I aspire to write as consistently well as Ron.

In this first collection you'll see that I am the kid at Xmas: excited and needing to play with all of the toys at once. Hence, *Soaring* contains many different styles and forms of poetry. In this and other aspects of my life, I hope never to grow up.

The cover photo of a white-bellied sea eagle was taken by Ford Kristo.

A great thrill for me these days is when Jeanie introduces me as 'Oh, this is my husband, he's a poet.'

'Wedding photos in the park' and 'Whazisname from the commuters' club' were published online by SCWC in conjunction with Wollongong City Council's Pole Poetry Project 2016.

'From the watchtower' was published in *Dreaming Inside – Voices from Junee Correctional Centre*, Volume 3, 2015.

'Helicopter' was published in *Seeking Horizons*, South Coast Writers Centre Anthology 2014.

'Oyster Bay' was winner of the Sydney Writers Festival Rocket Readings 2014.

'Saturday morning is all right' was third in the Sydney Writers Festival Rocket Readings 2016.

Lastly, I want to acknowledge the land, the life it provides and the reciprocity of kindliness

Sea eagle

…serene in my place
floating on a coastal breeze
soaring above the angst
a calm strength of mind and wing
for now…

www.ingramcontent.com/pod-product-compliance
Lightning Source LLC
Chambersburg PA
CBHW070911080526
44589CB00013B/1258